Earth's Changing Crust

Rebecca Harman

Heinemann Library
Chicago, Illinois

© Heinemann Library 2005
an imprint of Capstone Global Library, LLC
Chicago, Illinois

Customer Service 888-454-2279
Visit our website at www.heinemannlibrary.com

All rights reserved. No part of this publication may be reproduced, stored in a retrieval system,
or transmitted in any form or by any means, electronic, mechanical, photocopying, recording,
or otherwise, without the prior written permission of the Publisher.

Editorial: Melanie Copland
Design: Victoria Bevan and AMR Design
Illustration: Art Construction and
David Woodroffe
Picture Research: Mica Brancic and
Helen Reilly
Production: Duncan Gilbert

Originated by Chroma Graphics (Overseas) Pte. Ltd
Printed and bound in the United States of America, North Mankato, MN.

13 12 11
10 9 8 7 6 5 4 3

Library of Congress Cataloging-in-Publication Data

Harman, Rebecca.
   Earth's changing crust / Rebecca Harman.
      p. cm. -- (Earth's processes)
   Includes bibliographical references and index.
   ISBN 1-4034-7056-1 (lib. bdg.) -- ISBN 978-1-4034-7063-8 (pbk.)
   1. Earth--Crust--Juvenile literature. 2. Plate tectonics--Juvenile literature. I. Title. II. Series.
   QE511.H416 2005
   551.1'36--dc22

                                          2005010641

Acknowledgments

The Publishers would like to thank the following for permission to reproduce photographs:
Associated Press **pp. 23**; **24**;(Mike O'Neall), Corbis **pp. 26**, **28**; Geoscience Features **pp. 4**, **5**, **13**, **20**;
Rex Features Ltd **27**;(Sipa Press), Science Photo Library **pp. 15**;(NASA), **17**; (Will & Deni McIntyre),
22; (David Weintraub), **25**; (Space Imaging), Still Pictures **pp. 9**; (Arnold Newman),**16**; (Kevin
Schafer).

Cover photograph of the San Andreas Fault on Carrizo Plain, South California reproduced with
permission of Alamy.

The Publishers would like to thank Nick Lapthorn for his assistance in the preparation of this book.

Every effort has been made to contact copyright holders of any material reproduced in this
book. Any omissions will be rectified in subsequent printings if notice is given to the Publishers.

112011
006418RP

Contents

Words appearing in the text in bold, like this, are explained in the Glossary.

Is Earth's Surface Changing?

On November 14, 1963 a fishing boat in the Atlantic Ocean near Iceland reported a huge underwater explosion. This was caused by a **volcano** erupting under the sea. Smoke, steam, ash, and rocks exploded out above the ocean surface. A new island called Surtsey was made.

This is a dramatic example of how Earth's surface can change very quickly. We may think that Earth does not move, because most of the time we cannot see it moving. In fact, the whole of Earth's surface is always moving.

The island of Surtsey, southwest of Iceland, was created when an underwater volcano exploded.

The land areas where we live are called **continents**. They move very slowly – about 2.8 inches (7 centimeters) each year. Mountain ranges, such as the Alps in Europe, are rising. Waterfalls, such as Niagara Falls in North America, are wearing away the rocks behind them. These changes all take place so slowly that we cannot see them happening.

Sometimes Earth moves very quickly, such as during violent, explosive **earthquakes** or volcanic **eruptions**. The eruption that created the island of Surtsey is an example of Earth moving very quickly.

Did you know?

Earth is extremely old. It is 4,600 million years old, and its surface has been changing all this time. It is difficult to imagine something this old, so instead, we can get rid of all the zeros and pretend Earth is a 46-year-old person. We do not know anything about Earth until it was 40 years old. The dinosaurs appeared one year ago, when it was 45, and humans appeared 4 hours ago. The United States was discovered by a man called Columbus just 3 minutes ago, and the year 2000 happened only 2 seconds ago. So you can see there is a lot about the history of Earth that we do not know!

The Alps are rising, but too slowly for us to see it happening.

What is Earth's Crust?

The inside of Earth is like an onion. It is made up of different layers. The **crust** forms the surface layer. It is a very thin layer, like the skin of an onion. There are two types of crust, continental and oceanic. Continental crust can be up to $43\frac{1}{2}$ miles (70 kilometers) thick and is found beneath the continents. Oceanic crust is thinner—about 6 miles (10 kilometers) thick—but heavier than continental crust. It is found beneath the oceans.

What is below the crust?

If we could dig deep into the crust, we would eventually reach the **mantle**. This is a thick layer, starting at the base of the crust and going 1,802 miles (2,900 kilometers) deep into Earth. The rocks in the mantle are very hot, reaching up to 5,432°F (3,000 °C) and partly **molten** (melted).

The **core** forms the middle of Earth. It can be separated into the outer core (which is liquid) and the inner core (which is solid).

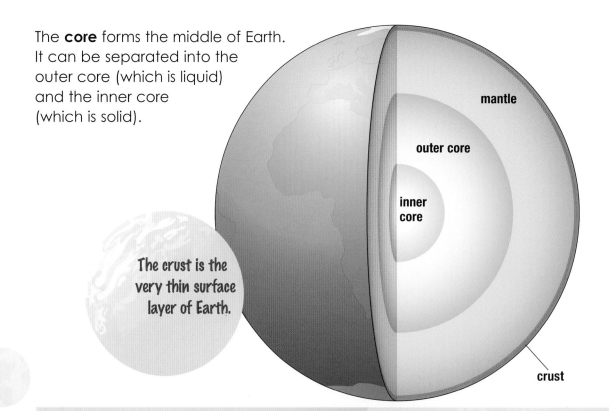

mantle

outer core

inner core

crust

The crust is the very thin surface layer of Earth.

Is the crust broken into pieces?

Earth's crust is not one solid layer. It is broken up into huge, moving pieces called **plates** that fit together like a giant jigsaw puzzle. The plates are rigid (stiff), and float like rafts on the mantle below. Some of the plates are very large, such as the Pacific Plate, which lies beneath the whole of the Pacific Ocean.

Does the crust move?

The plates move very slowly over Earth – up to 4 inches (10 centimeters) per year. Although they move slowly, they are moving all the time, carrying the continents and oceans with them. This is called **plate tectonics**. The movements of the plates cause most of the big changes that take place on the surface of Earth. Nearly all of the volcanoes in the world are found at the edges of the plates. The edges of the plates are called **plate boundaries**.

Earth's crust is broken up into huge plates that move slowly across the Earth's surface.

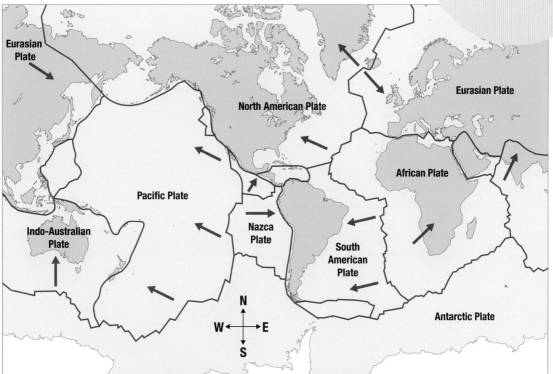

Eurasian Plate

Eurasian Plate

North American Plate

African Plate

Pacific Plate

Nazca Plate

Indo-Australian Plate

South American Plate

Antarctic Plate

N
W ← → E
S

How Do We Know the Continents Move?

Geology is the study of rocks. **Geologists** are like detectives. They need to look at lots of different clues to work out what has happened to Earth in the past. They have found clues that show the continents used to be joined together, but have slowly moved apart over millions of years.

The shape of the coastlines of eastern South America and west Africa appear to fit together like a jigsaw puzzle. This means that they may have been joined together at one time, and then moved apart.

Geologists think that many places on Earth had different weather conditions or **climates** in the past, so these places used to be much colder or warmer. For example, scratches in rocks in Australia, India, South America, and Africa are thought to have been made by moving ice. The clues show that these lands used to lie over the South Pole, and some parts were covered in ice.

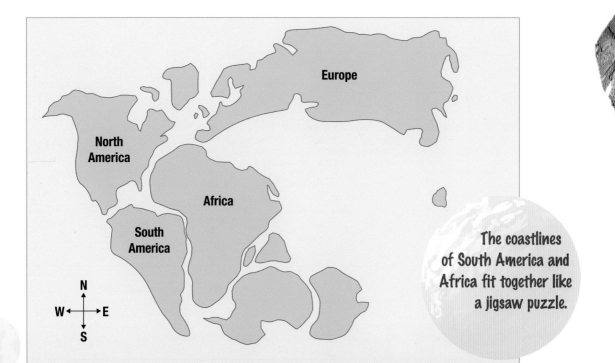

The coastlines of South America and Africa fit together like a jigsaw puzzle.

Matching rocks are found in other places, such as Scotland and Canada. This means that they may have been joined together in the past. These countries are now on opposite sides of the Atlantic Ocean.

The same **fossils** are found in lands now separated by oceans. For example, fossils of the same reptile are found in Brazil and South Africa. This means that when the animal was alive, it could wander around both countries, and so the countries must once have been joined together.

All these clues show that the continents have slowly moved apart through time. This is called **continental drift**.

Fossils of a crocodile-like reptile have been found in both Brazil and South Africa. These countries are now separated by the Atlantic Ocean.

How has the Continental Jigsaw Puzzle Changed?

Continents are the large land areas on which we live. Today there are seven main continents on Earth: North America, South America, Europe, Asia, Australia, Africa, and Antarctica. This has not always been the case. In the past all the continents were joined together to form one giant **supercontinent**.

About 200 million years ago, there was just one supercontinent called Pangaea. Around 160 million years ago, Pangaea started to break up. This was when dinosaurs lived on Earth. Pangaea split in two, and a new ocean was created that became wider over time. The two new continents were called Gondwanaland (made up of South America, Africa, India, Antarctica, and Australia) and Laurasia (made up of North America, Europe, and Asia). These two continents then split up again into the continents we have today.

The Atlantic Ocean started to form 120 million years ago when the continent of Laurasia split in two. Today the Atlantic Ocean is still getting wider by about $1\frac{1}{2}$ inches (4 centimeters) per year.

Did you know?

India crashed violently against the Eurasian plate about 50 million years ago. The land squashed together and created the Himalaya Mountains. This movement is still happening and the Himalayas continue to get higher.

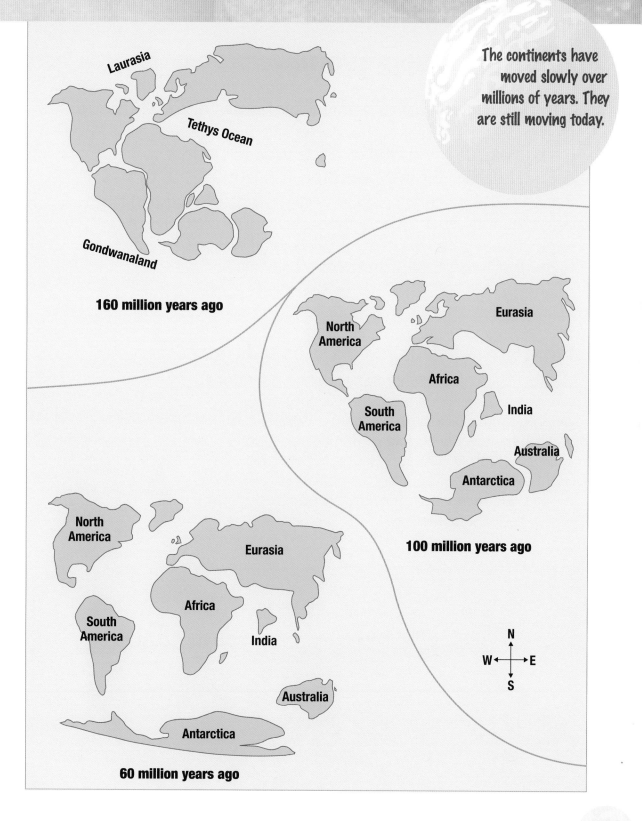

Laurasia

Tethys Ocean

Gondwanaland

160 million years ago

The continents have moved slowly over millions of years. They are still moving today.

North America

Eurasia

Africa

South America

India

Australia

Antarctica

100 million years ago

North America

Eurasia

Africa

South America

India

Australia

Antarctica

N
W E
S

60 million years ago

How Do Plates Move?

The main driving force behind plate movement is thought to be a system that works like a giant conveyor belt. Molten rock (**magma**) from the mantle rises to Earth's surface at a **constructive plate boundary**. This pushes the plates apart, causing them to move. The magma cools to form new crust. As this crust moves away from the plate boundary, it becomes thicker and heavier. As it moves toward a **destructive plate boundary**, it sinks into the mantle and pulls the rest of the plate behind it.

What are constructive plate boundaries?

Constructive plate boundaries are plate boundaries where new crust is created. They usually occur along giant mountain chains on the ocean floor. These are called **mid ocean ridges**. One example is the Mid Atlantic Ridge in the middle of the Atlantic Ocean. The two plates move away from each other through a process called **seafloor spreading**.

As two plates move apart at a mid ocean ridge, new magma rises to fill the gap, so new seafloor is created.

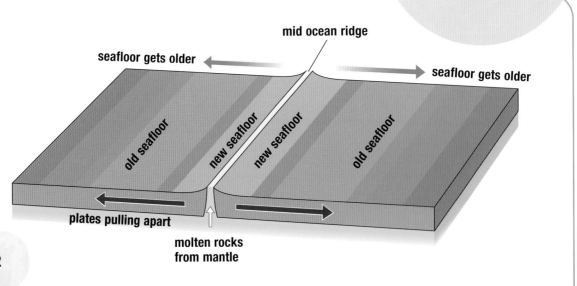

mid ocean ridge

seafloor gets older ←   → seafloor gets older

old seafloor   new seafloor   new seafloor   old seafloor

plates pulling apart

molten rocks from mantle

Did you know?

Iceland forms part of the Mid Atlantic Ridge, where the underwater mountains are so high they reach above the surface of the ocean. Iceland is growing from the middle outwards, and is entirely built from **lava**, just like the rest of the Mid Atlantic Ridge.

The Mid Atlantic Ridge is a constructive plate boundary. This is a smoking volcano on the ridge, deep underwater.

During seafloor spreading, molten rock from the mantle oozes to the surface (as **lava**) to form new seafloor, pushing the plates apart. The new crust spreads outwards from both sides of the ridge very slowly, at a rate of less than an inch per year (the same rate that fingernails grow). The spreading of the Mid Atlantic Ridge is slowly pushing Europe and North America farther away from each other. As the crust gradually moves away from the constructive plate boundary, it becomes older, colder, and heavier.

What are destructive plate boundaries?

If new crust is made at constructive plate boundaries, the same amount of crust must also be destroyed somewhere else. Otherwise Earth would get bigger and bigger! The places where crust is destroyed are called destructive plate boundaries. This type of boundary forms where two plates move toward each other, such as on the west coast of South America.

Crust formed at a mid ocean ridge slowly moves away from the constructive plate boundary. Over millions of years, it becomes old, cold, thick, and heavy. When the crust meets another plate, at a destructive plate boundary, it plunges down into a deep valley in the ocean floor, called an **ocean trench**. The Marianas Trench in the Pacific Ocean is an ocean trench. It goes deep into the mantle where it melts. This is called **subduction**. Oceanic crust always sinks under continental crust, because oceanic crust is heavier. When the crust slides into the mantle, it causes **friction** (rubbing). This results in earthquakes on the continent next to the ocean trench.

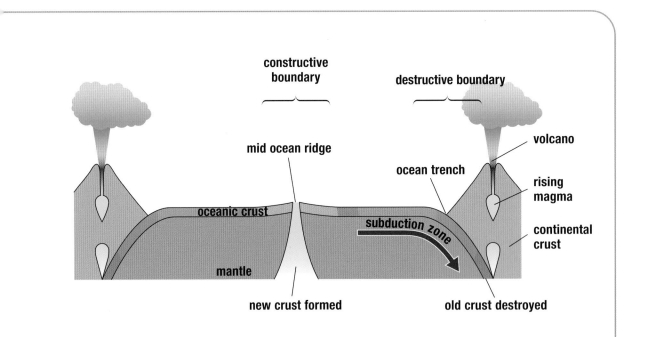

Marianas
Trench

Mid Atlantic
Ridge

These maps of the
ocean floor show where
mid ocean ridges and
ocean trenches
are found.

What Landforms are Found at Plate Boundaries?

Over millions of years, Earth's surface is changed by plate tectonics. All of Earth's biggest landforms, such as mountains, volcanoes, and ocean trenches, are formed by plate movements.

What landforms are found at constructive plate boundaries?

Long chains of volcanoes are found at mid ocean ridges, such as the Mid Atlantic Ridge and the East Pacific Rise in the eastern Pacific Ocean. These volcanoes are usually underwater, but Iceland forms a part of the Mid Atlantic Ridge where the volcanoes rise above sea level.

Steam and smoke rise from mountains in the Mid Atlantic Ridge on Iceland.

What landforms are found at destructive plate boundaries?

As crust sinks down into the mantle, it melts and then rises toward Earth's surface, in the same way as blobs rise in a lava lamp. This movement thickens the crust and produces chains of mountains and volcanoes along destructive plate boundaries. The best example of such a chain of volcanoes is the Andes mountain range that stretches for the entire length of the west coast of South America.

On the oceanward side of the chain of volcanoes, a destructive plate boundary has an ocean trench. The Marianas Trench in the Pacific Ocean is one example. Ocean trenches are deep, underwater valleys on the seafloor.

Did you know?

The Marianas Trench in the Pacific Ocean is the deepest place on Earth. It is 7 miles (11 kilometers) deep. That is deep enough to swallow Mount Everest!

The Andes mountain range marks the position of a destructive plate boundary.

What Other Types of Plate Boundaries are There?

There are many other types of plate boundaries. Transform and collision boundaries are the most common.

What are transform boundaries?

Transform boundaries are where two plates slide past each other along a **transform fault**. At these boundaries crust is neither created nor destroyed. The plates do not slide past each other smoothly, but in a series of jerks. These can result in earthquakes.

The most famous example is the San Andreas Fault, in California. Here the Pacific Plate grinds north past the North American Plate at about 2 inches (5 centimeters) per year. Sometimes the two plates slip past each other in a sudden movement, resulting in violent earthquakes. The last major earthquake in this region happened in 1994 when 61 people were killed.

The cities of San Francisco and Los Angeles are very close to the San Andreas Fault. This means that they are at risk from earthquakes.

Did you know?

In around 10 million years time Los Angeles will be where San Francisco is now. This is because the Pacific Plate is moving north.

N
W E
S

CANADA

NORTH AMERICAN PLATE

San Francisco

San Andreas Fault

Los Angeles

PACIFIC PLATE

UNITED STATES

Pacific Ocean

MEXICO

0   500km

What are collision boundaries?

Collision boundaries occur when two continents run into each other, or collide, like in a car crash. However, this happens in very slow motion, over millions of years.

When two continents collide, mountain ranges are produced as Earth's crust is squashed in between the plates and is pushed upward. The ocean between the colliding continents drains away, and material from the old ocean floor is pushed up high into the new mountains. As a result fossils of sea creatures can be found high in the mountains.

India collided with Asia about 50 million years ago, forming the Himalayas.

ASIA

Himalayas

Present

20 million years ago

40 million years ago

60 million years ago

INDIA

80 million years ago

0   1000 miles
          1609.2 km

N
W ← → E
S

Between about 80 and 50 million years ago, the Indian plate began moving toward Asia at a rate of 4 to 8 inches (10 to 20 centimeters) per year. About 50 million years ago, the Indian Plate collided with Asia, and the crust in-between was squashed together to form the Himalayas. The Indian Plate is still moving north today, but at a slower rate than before. It now moves about 2 inches (5 centimeters) per year. This means the Himalayas are still getting higher.

The Himalayas are the youngest mountains on Earth. They contain Mount Everest, the highest mountain in the world.

What are Extreme Events?

Plate tectonics and continental drift happen very slowly over millions of years. But some processes on Earth can happen very suddenly, and are called **extreme events**. They include volcanic eruptions and earthquakes. People have very little control over these events. Their impact is sudden, and they can occur with very little warning. These extreme events are not evenly spread across Earth's surface. They mainly happen at plate boundaries.

Where do volcanic eruptions happen?

Most volcanoes are found at plate boundaries, either along mid ocean ridges (constructive boundaries) or where one plate moves beneath another at a subduction zone (destructive boundaries). The eruption in 1991 of Pinatubo in the Philippines happened at a subduction zone. Most of the volcanoes in the world are found in a ring around the Pacific Ocean, called the **Ring of Fire**.

This map shows the Pacific Ring of Fire. These volcanoes are all found along subduction zones. Many major earthquakes happen here.

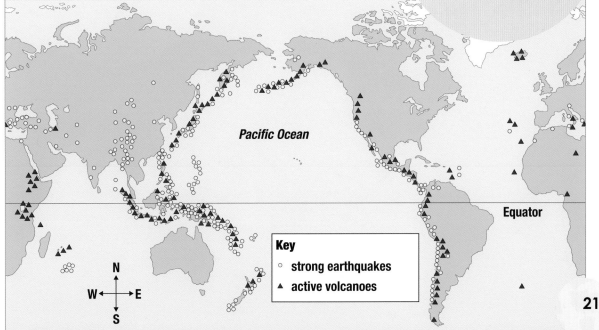

Pacific Ocean

Equator

Key

○ strong earthquakes

▲ active volcanoes

N

W ← → E

S

Some volcanoes are always erupting, while others may be quiet for hundreds of years and then suddenly burst into action. The town of Pompeii in Italy was wiped out by the sudden eruption of a volcano called Vesuvius in AD 79. Most people in Pompeii did not even realize Vesuvius was a volcano because it had not erupted for many years. Mount St. Helens in the state of Washington suddenly came back to life in 1980 after 123 years.

The violence of a volcanic eruption is caused by the type of lava that is thrown out. Runny lava runs quickly and quietly over Earth's surface. This is produced by volcanoes along mid ocean ridges. Thick lava is more explosive as it has gas trapped in it. This explodes when it erupts out of the volcano and produces clouds of ash. Krakatoa is a volcano in southeast Asia that erupted so violently in 1883 that it blew itself apart.

Did you know?

There are over 3,000 active volcanoes scattered across Earth's surface, and about 50 volcanoes are likely to erupt each year.

The explosion of Krakatoa in 1883 was much more violent than this volcanic eruption.

What are earthquakes?

Earthquakes are caused when plates suddenly slide past each other at a transform boundary or when the crust slides into the mantle at a destructive plate boundary. The friction caused by both of these processes causes a build-up of pressure in the crust. When this pressure is suddenly released, parts of Earth's surface will shake.

Luckily for humans most earthquakes are too small to be noticed. But some are powerful enough to flatten entire cities, killing the people who live in them. In 2001 an earthquake in India killed about 20,000 people.

There was a devastating earthquake in southeast Iran on December 26, 2003. Many buildings and roads were destroyed, and 30,000 people lost their lives.

Huge cracks in the ground can happen as a result of an earthquake, like this one in San Francisco in 1906.

Did you know?

Earthquakes shake the surface of Earth over half a million times a year. This adds up to one earthquake every minute! Most of them are very small or happen far away from towns and cities, so people are not usually affected.

What are landslides and mudslides?

When earthquakes strike in hilly or mountainous areas, they might trigger **landslides** and **mudslides**. A landslide is caused when huge chunks of rock and soil on the mountain slopes suddenly slide very quickly, crashing down the hillside. An earthquake on October 23, 2004 in Japan, just north of Tokyo, caused 150 landslides because the area is very hilly.

Mudslides occur when ash thrown out from a volcano mixes with water to form a fast-flowing river of mud. In 1985 in Colombia, an ice-covered volcano called Nevado del Ruiz blasted hot ash and gas across the ice, causing it to melt. This created a huge mudslide that poured down the mountainside.

Mudslides can happen so quickly that they bury everything in their path.

What are tsunamis?

Tsunamis are huge sea waves caused by earthquakes, landslides, or volcanic eruptions underwater. The waves travel through water at the same speed as a jet plane travels through the air. This means they can cross an entire ocean in a few hours, bringing death and destruction to people thousands of miles away. The height of the waves can reach up to 131 feet (40 meters). They can damage buildings and tear away soil and rocks.

On December 26, 2004, an underwater earthquake in the Indian Ocean caused a tsunami to strike the coasts of Indonesia, Malaysia, Thailand, Myanmar, India, Sri Lanka, the Maldives, and Somalia. More than 280,000 people were killed. The water destroyed towns and villages, and millions were left homeless.

This satellite image shows a huge area of coast in Thailand that was flooded by the 2004 tsunami. The area that was flooded appears light brown.

How Do Extreme Events Affect People?

Extreme events cause problems when they occur in places where a lot of people live. As the population of the world increases, more people are living near plate boundaries, so more people are affected by extreme events.

How do volcanic eruptions affect people?

Hot, runny lava from an erupting volcano travels quickly, destroying everything in its path, including crops, roads, bridges, and buildings. Thicker lava travels more slowly, and does not cause as much damage. Both types of lava flows rarely cause death because people have time to get out of the way.

Explosive eruptions can be much more devastating if they affect places where many people live. When Vesuvius erupted in Italy in AD 79, a huge blast of ash, rocks, and gas covered the town of Pompeii. More than 2,000 people were killed instantly.

In Pompeii the bodies of people have been preserved as plastercasts made in the volcanic ash, after the eruption of Vesuvius in AD 79.

How do earthquakes affect people?

Earthquakes cause buildings to fall down, electricity and telephone wires to snap, and water and gas pipes to burst. When an earthquake strikes a big city, most deaths are caused by this kind of destruction, rather than the shaking of Earth itself. The 2003 earthquake in Iran killed 30,000 people, as old buildings crumbled.

How do landslides and mudslides affect people?

Landslides and mudslides travel very quickly over long distances. In 1985 in Colombia, a huge mudslide poured down a mountain into the town of Armero. The people who lived there could not escape, and they were buried under a thick blanket of mud. Over 23,000 people were killed.

How do tsunamis affect people?

Tsunamis cause flooding and water damage in coastal areas. The 2004 tsunami in the Indian Ocean completely destroyed many of the coastal villages it struck, particularly in Indonesia, Sri Lanka, Thailand, and India.

When large numbers of people live near an earthquake zone, large numbers of people will be affected.

STOP

Conclusion

Throughout history Earth's surface has been changing. It is always moving, in some places so slowly that we do not notice, and in other places so quickly that it takes us by surprise.

New crust is always being created at constructive plate boundaries, and crust is always being destroyed at destructive plate boundaries. This sets up the cycle of movement that causes most of the changes that take place on Earth's surface. Sometimes plates slide past each other and sometimes they crash together, pushing up huge mountain ranges.

The movements of the plates occur very slowly over millions of years. Spectacular events along the boundaries of plates, such as volcanic eruptions and earthquakes, happen much faster. As the population of the world increases, more people are living near plate boundaries, so more people are affected by these extreme events. It is important to understand about these events so that we can predict when they might happen and warn the people who will be affected.

Earth's surface is always changing.

Fact File

The world's ten largest volcanic eruptions.

Year	Volcano	Place	Deaths
1995	Soufriere Hills	Montserrat	20
1991	Pinatubo	Philippines	800
1982	El Chichon	Mexico	2,000
1980	Mount St. Helens	United States	57
1902	Mont Pelee	Martinique	28,000
1912	Novarupta	Alaska	2
1886	Tarawera	New Zealand	150
1875	Askja	Iceland	0
1883	Krakatoa	Indonesia	36,000
1815	Tambora	Indonesia	92,000

The world's ten deadliest earthquakes.

Year	Place	Deaths
2004	Indian Ocean	280,000
2003	Iran	30,000
2001	India	20,000
1999	Turkey	19,000
1995	Japan	6,000
1993	India	10,000
1990	Iran	50,000
1988	Armenia	25,000
1985	Mexico	10,000
1976	China	290,000

Glossary

climate type of weather an area usually experiences

collision boundary place where two continents crash together

constructive plate boundary area where two plates move apart and new crust is created

continent large area of land

continental drift movement of continents over time

core central layer of Earth

crust thin surface layer of Earth

destructive plate boundary area where two plates meet and crust is destroyed as one plate sinks beneath the other

earthquake shaking of the ground

eruption event when a volcano throws out lava or ash violently or suddenly

extreme event event that happens suddenly, such as an earthquake

fossil remains of a dead plant or animal

friction when two surfaces get stuck as they try to slide past each other

geologist scientist who studies Earth and the rocks it is made of

Gondwanaland southern part of Pangaea

landslide river of rocks flowing down a mountain very quickly

Laurasia northern part of Pangaea

lava name for magma when it reaches Earth's surface

magma hot rock from below Earth's surface

mantle hot layer of Earth beneath the crust

mid ocean ridge line of mountains on the seafloor

molten melted

mudslide river of ash and water flowing very quickly

ocean trench deep valley in the ocean floor found at destructive plate boundaries

Pangaea supercontinent made of the seven present-day continents

plate giant, moving piece of crust

plate boundary edge of a plate, where one plate meets another

plate tectonics movement of the plates across Earth

predict say what will happen in the future

Ring of Fire circle of volcanoes surrounding the Pacific Ocean

seafloor spreading the way that plates move apart at a constructive plate boundary

subduction one plate sliding beneath another at a destructive plate boundary

supercontinent giant area of land made of a number of continents joined together

transform boundary area where two plates slide past each other

transform fault crack in the crust where two plates slide past each other

tsunami huge sea wave caused by an underwater earthquake, landslide, or volcanic eruption

volcano mountain containing hot magma that erupts as lava from time to time

More books to read

Oxlade, Chris. *Earth's Changing Landscape: Earthquakes and Volcanoes.* Minnesota: Smart Apple Media, 2004.

Stewart, Melissa. *Soil (Rocks & Minerals series).* Chicago: Heinemann Library, 2002.

Townsend, John. *Earthquakes and Volcanoes.* Chicago: Raintree, 2005.

Index